LIFE, IN SHORTS

Poems by Rachel Davies

First published 2024

© Rachel Davies, 2024

The right of Rachel Davies to be identified as author of this work
has been asserted in accordance with section 77 of the Copyright,
Designs and Patents Act 1988.

ISBN 978-1-0685815-0-2

A catalogue record for this book is available from the British Library.

Cover Art by Natasha Evans.
https://natashaevansart.com

Typesetting by Sheer Book Design
www.sheerbookdesign.com

CONTENTS

INTRODUCTION

I applied to volunteer with Voluntary Services Overseas (VSO) in 2007, and eagerly waited to find out what my placement would be and where in the world I would be moving to. I had no idea where Zambia was, or what to expect, but I packed my bags, moved to Siavonga, and by the time I returned to London over a year later, I realised I'd left part of my heart there.

Many years later, I came back to Siavonga with my husband and children, and we decided to spend a year in Lusaka.

I started writing these poems as a way of processing what I was experiencing throughout our move. It felt like a helpful way of recording this very different life, watching my children tossing their shoes and running barefoot, holding onto the side of cars with the wind in their hair, and spending their days playing outdoors with some rope, sticks and their imaginations. It gave me so much joy. Through exploring place and being away from home, I was also reflecting on what home means: identity, parenting, difference, privilege and inequality. These themes run throughout the poems.

My hope is that this collection offers a small insight into what it means to be outside our comfort zone, and that this might encourage all of us, myself included, to explore more.

Whenever I've travelled, I've always been struck by how good people are. In sharing this, I hope to share that optimism and positivity about the world and who we are as humans.

LIFE, IN SHORTS

There was a time when we made our home
at the end of a road with dust and potholes.
Surrounded by trees – some guarded by thorns the length
   of your finger,
some that dropped lemons, limes, avocados, guava;
two goats, and next door, peacocks that appeared
on top of the highest bushes;
chameleons that pranced,
and light that danced through the windows
onto polished concrete floors.

IF THIS WAS YOUR PLAYGROUND

Imagine if this was your playground –
the space, the freedom,
trees to climb, and piles of building sand
to catch your fall;

chickens to snatch and cuddle,
lizards, snakes, baby birds in the trees.
Bush babies, eyes glinting in the dark,
and more stars than you could ever count.

If you have just a rope and some ways to tie it,
you can have a swing, a raft,
a time-travelling machine.

If you're by the water
and someone looks out for crocs,
the whole day can pass by
beautifully.

An inner pen tube, a clothes peg wire –
you have a rocket launcher.
So little,
but everything

and as you stand on a pile of rocks and leap into the air,
rays of the setting sun catching the top of your hair,
there is nowhere else in the world
you could ever hope to be
but here.

ZESCO

No power again
feels like a good experience
for two children born and raised in London.
We scurry to our beds with torches,
snuggle up in pitch black, inside and out.
No lights, no internet,
no fridge or freezer.
Running water for now,
but once the water pump stops,
the water stops too.

Opening birthday presents by torchlight
in front of the fire,
appreciating what we have –
there is no price to be put
on that.

THE LAKE

I arrived at the lake when I was young and alone,
delivered at Hill Top on crutches
with no way down but to limp,
so I did.

I discovered a sanctuary of calm,
kapenta and Bloody Marys,
watching the sun set over the lake.
Those sunsets are
indescribable.
Just when you think
it couldn't get more beautiful,
the colours intensify:
fiery oranges and reds,
candy pinks reflecting on the water,
becoming more beautiful still.

I found my feet
literally – my foot healed.
Crutches donated
and then friends, purpose,
enough Tonga to ease my difference,
share a smile,
and it became another home.

We drive in.
My 7 year old rolls down the window.
"Why do the fires smell
so much better here?
It smells like home."

THE SNAKE WHISPERER

When I first came to Zambia
I worried about snakes.
They sensed my energy –
I called them.
They appeared in places
no one had seen a snake
in years.

It's true what they say –
your mouth gasps "Oh",
involuntarily;
you float up and back
without conscious effort,
then freeze,
heart thumping
in your throat.

I had to change my energy.
My new mantra became
She never saw a snake again.
I chanted it to myself
as I walked
along grassy paths
or unlit roads, and
I don't want to jinx anything –
there have been those small
road snakes
in the daytime,
at a distance –
but so far
it's working,
for now.

HOME

Who am I in a place far from home,
where I find myself asking what home really is?
We're so connected, I could be down the road
but I am here – sunshine, warmth,
mukuyu, marula, mopane and sausage trees,
green shimmering dragonflies swooping in laps around the garden,
people who greet you in the street,
children who run with bare feet –
there's less, also much more, and it's so different.
Home is where you make it.
Home takes time, it climbs into your heart –
small pieces add to what was there before,
to what we become.
I'll carry this with me to the next,
and the next.

SPECIAL OCCASIONS

The giraffe at the end of the road
comes out for special occasions:
our arrival (although we thought that was normal),
and when we need a little boost.
Its mottled, deep brown pattern
is perfectly camouflaged in the dry, long grasses,
brown, thorny trees, and scrub,
and can only have been designed
by something with a
wild imagination.

LIFE

The crow of the cockerel
as the grasshoppers chirrup,
a sound mind-breakingly loud
for their small bodies.
A leaf falls. The sun tickles
the tops of the trees, moving slowly
to cast its light across the grass path,
rays caressing everything they touch
before the later scorch –
the burn in the heat of the day – but gentle now.
Soft early morning, as the dreams
of a billion creatures float in the air.
Centuries of life on life on
red earth. Dust.

SMELL

Wood smoke,
earth,
dust,
damp ground,
rain on hot earth,
fresh, green vegetation,
cars spewing black smoke,
tyres skid,
burnt rubber,
jacaranda flowers heavy with perfume,
ripe guava on the tree,
fires burning,
soap,
freshly washed bodies,
sour, stale sweat,
sun-baked,
big outdoors,
dung,
smoke,
death,
life,
alive.

THE VILLAGE

They danced –
the women, the men, and the children.
Strong hands beat rhythms on the drums
and they sang in harmony:
hips swaying, joy radiating through the air.
We got up too, and they laughed and laughed.
The sun beat down through the branches,
the dust rose, and the chicken that had been squawking
a little while ago was almost ready,
as was the goat, with nshima and relish.
And we continued dancing, even though our common language
was nothing more than a few words.

The water pump is too far,
so we have to carry heavy buckets of water.
There's drought. We don't know if we'll have enough food.
We're scared. But the school is good.
We want more. More classrooms, more teachers.
We want our children to always learn here,
where they're given food and a good education,
and don't have to walk for more than an hour to school.

We dream of more – of a better life,
but for now,
we dance.

GLOW WORM

When I was very young I had a glow worm, plastic,
with a purple sleeping bag and
sleeping hat falling to one side,
a green glow,
my treasure.

I didn't know then that nature
could be even more beautiful than the
plastic glow worm I reluctantly threw away
after 35 years.

Now one shines like a tiny lightbulb
on the path, between the stones by the wall –
a luminous green worm's tail,
brighter than should be naturally possible.
Luminous,
small,
alive.
A miracle.

KNOWING

I know this feeling not because I've lived it,
but because it's in my blood, my veins,
my nervous system.
So now we can be on the alert, ears
pricked, sniff the wind – are they coming for us?
"Don't put your money into buying
a piano," my mother said.
"You can't pick it up, or take it with you when you run."
When will we run again – is it now?
Did you smell it on the wind,
or do we have a little more time?

I feel it in my bones.
There's an early warning system:
smoke signals, fires on the hills.
They knew when to get out –
the ones who lived. They knew
the *safe-havens*, from the *not-safe-for-much-longer* places,
and it's in my cells to look out.
Is it coming, or is there still time?

WHERE ARE YOU FROM?

You can't place me,
can't place my face,
can't see the Russian steppes,
cold wind, or the Lithuanian shtetls –
people fleeing the land to wander,
to set down roots and then move on.
Don't you recognise my face from Germany –
the curve of my brow,
the deep-set eyes of the merchants asking the ruler
for permission to leave the village?
Is there some Italian, or Spanish,
from communities hiding their identity
for fear of being killed, perhaps?
The sun made its mark,
and a gene found in the Mediterranean.
I tan, golden-bronzed skin.
Where am I from?
What can't you place
about my face?

SADNESS

"There's a sadness in you. I can feel it" she said,
after she removed the brass bowl
from my head.
Strange… I thought I hid it so well.
My people are at war,
are losing the PR war,
perhaps the whole war,
and it's not safe to say out loud
that I'm scared
for my family,
my extended family,
and the home I hope I won't need.
But with every passing week I wonder,
when we'll need the land.

Safe,
keep them safe,
please, keep us all safe.

GRIPPING

What would it take to relax my shoulders,
clenched jaw, tongue, stomach,
allow it all to settle, spill over?
My mind is gripping too,
holding tightly onto *what ifs* and *what nows*.
What would it take to let that go too?
Even to let go of "Be present,
make the most of this time and this moment."

Can we be like the tide?
Ebb and flow, the waves,
without edges or questions,
overflowing,
rocking,
melting all tension away.

MATEMWE, ZANZIBAR

Whose story do we tell?
Which frame, what's in focus, and what's behind the lens?
Who can tell us about this moment?
A beach framed by tall palm trees,
a breeze, fine white sand,
the salty spray of the ocean.
Sea – shallow at first, turquoise,
with darker blue depths, calm ripples,
a steady white foam where the reef breaks.
Crows perch photogenically on a wooden dhow.
A child wades, holding a rope,
carefully securing a small boat to a red buoy.
Local children kick a football barefoot,
using weathered wooden poles for goals.
My son, face flushed from a day under the sun,
digs in the sand – focus, concentration,
sand flying up behind him.
And a woman, me, watching where the sunlight falls,
taking it all in, holding this moment light like a bubble;
choosing to stay here in the calm, the crash of the waves,
when everything outside this moment is unknown.
So much fear,
but this moment,
while the bubble holds,
is perfect, intact, whole.

ZESCO II

She ran.
How did she know what was happening,
as the electricity supply for the entire street
ran through his small body?
They picked him from the neatly mown grass.
I drove his barefoot mother.
They treated him, he was alive.
My mistake was Googling what might still be –
internal damage.
So much damage. They don't pay damages,
not even the medicine we gave his father money for.
Within hours, men arrived to fix the transformer.
In days the boy, Promise – who loved to ride bikes
side-saddle in a Christmas elf top, jeans short and torn,
and a grin to make your heart melt,
was carried by his father across the scrub,
too painful to walk, but better as time passed.
That smile returned.
Imagine all the children playing,
who aren't even statistics
because there are no
recorded damages.

PRECIOUS

We turned off the main road
onto a paved single track,
shacks on either side selling tomatoes,
bread, salt, cooking oil.
A restaurant in a single room,
charcoal brazier outside, aluminum cooking pot, lid on.
Women with babies on their backs
wrapped in colourful chitenge.
Children playing, holding hands, laughing.
Men walking, watching.
Hair being braided.
Music playing –
life.

We turned and stopped
by a green gate in front of uneven stones,
raised concrete platforms and open doors.
"This is home," she said,
with a half smile, embarrassed.
"Our small kitchen, the living room, two bedrooms,
the children are in that one.
The bathroom is outside."

She knew,
because she saw every day
how we amass possessions we don't need,
leave food to go limp, grow mould,
then throwing it away without a care.
How we spend money – a day's earnings,
on a piece of cheese.

And here she was, in these simple rooms
with red polished floors,
where everything was repaired and mended
and fixed and cared for –
nothing wasted and nothing taken for granted.
She knew.

ZAMBEZI

There is a river
in the place where the heat ripples;
it flows and flows,
sometimes full and strong,
flush with the rains,
and drier, lower now this year,
but still steel blue and grey,
shimmering iridescence as the eddy flows backwards,
gently drifting upstream.
Hippo ears, tops of heads, appear
and are gone.
Sink into the depths,
feel the flow, deep and slow
as the eddy carries you back around.
Slowly, slowly,
past golden green banks, bird chatter,
and a fish eagle perched on the top of the highest branches.
When you meet you'll continue,
slow and steady,
past rapids, fishermen on wooden canoes,
to the thundering waterfall.
Down, down,
then sink into the depths again.

IMPOSSIBLY BEAUTIFUL

Why do we say impossibly beautiful?
What is impossible?
Here, it's possible
that if you thought
of the most, the best,
the number one most incredible sunset
the world has ever witnessed,
it wouldn't match this.
This is more —
the light,
glow,
luminous,
luminescence,
from the horizon moving upwards;
yellow, then mauve haze punctuating purple,
through to indigo clouds catching the light
around their soft edges.
Now deep, pinky-orange glowing on the horizon,
becoming highlighter pink.
How can you even describe the temporary wonder,
suspended for a moment in time,
before it is gone?

WINDOW SHOPPING

On the road to Siavonga I could have bought
cobs of maize roasted over charcoal,
woven straw chicken houses,
a live chicken, wings held in a tight grip,
rocks in varying sizes in neat piles,
a homemade catapult;

tomatoes,
onions,
orange pumpkins,
watermelon,
sweet potato,
tall bags of black charcoal,
stacks of firewood,
sugarcane sprouting green leaves,
hacked into small pieces with a machete if you prefer;

reed matting with a black patterned design,
a metal brazier,
solid hardwood bed frames,
wooden giraffes,
woven reed baskets,
plants, seedlings in soil, in repurposed bags of cement;

animal skin drums,
wooden pestle and mortars varying in size,
jerry cans of petrol, with the price on painted signs,
fresh fish from the Kafue River in plastic bowls,
children offering up bags of masau fruit and groundnuts,
baobab fruit you crack open with a rock,
chunks of amethyst the size of my head.

Three hours, and all without getting up from my seat.

MUTINONDO (A TRUE STORY)

She saw the lioness' pawprints on the dusty path
pointing straight ahead
and back again,
both ways.
"She must have been and gone a while ago"
she said out loud
to no one.
It was only later,
after her beautiful walk amongst the hills,
the plain stretching wide and long,
baboons calling as the sun got lower,
(shadows lengthening and cooling the air, so lovely!)
and the cold stream running, gurgling over the rocks
like it always did,
that she discovered the lioness had circled a rock
and another set of footprints
had followed her
all the way home.

100 KWACHA

In an unpredictable system
consequences can be insignificant
or enormous.
Our road tax had expired.
I didn't know.
I paid 100 Kwacha, I drove on.
Money in her pocket, a story to tell.
When you take away the rule book,
put power in people's hands
to earn a little money on the side,
it's impossible to predict what happens next.
She threatened court.
She threatened fines.
My heart beat fast as I took deep, slow breaths.
A little money smoothed it all over.
As I sat in the back of the police car weighing it up –
principles, yes.
It's also nice to walk away.

JUNE

When the sun shines
and makes shadows
in the shape of palm branches
that lie
across the table,
across my face –
we're caressed by silhouettes that dance and sway.
The sun will rise each day.
It rises,
coaxes the shadows into being,
creating shapes that gently kiss the curtains –
consistent,
reliable,
hopeful –
warmth and beauty giving life and growth.
In a world full of uncertainty,
I know that the sun will rise
to make shadows that sway
and warm tired bones.

CHAWAMA

Steaming piles of rubbish, trash,
plastic
for miles.
Children, adults, sit, move, work
on steaming piles
where it all goes,
all ends up on this long railway track
to the end of the world.
Children leap, perch, collect in bags,
sit, stare.
We don't know,
don't care,
don't dare to care
what their day, their week,
their life will be.
What stories under the stories
lie waiting to pounce, tear at our hearts.

POLICE

Headlights flash, one after another after another
from the other side of the road as I drive –
vehicles communicating across the concrete barrier that divides it,
and that people step over with children,
giant baskets on their heads,
or bicycles lifted over as cars whip by.
Then I see what they were telling me,
as ten enormous black speed cameras
on tripods, all in a row, come into view;
police behind each camera pointed at the cars, at me.
I feel like the paparazzi are waiting for me –
so many police, they must be in training.
A flock, a flurry, a herd.
I've already slowed down
and I smile, driving free,
like in the bush –
the hunters, the hunted,
and the birds squawking their alarm call,
an early warning system –
we're on the same team.

GLIMPSES

Never underestimate the power
of being out of your comfort zone –
of being in another world
and taking glimpses inside,
where the mundane for other people
feels joyful,
eyes wide with wonder –
"What's over there?
What are they doing?
Did you see that?"
How am I so lucky,
to have a glimpse
of this sunset,
this road,
these people,
these lives I don't fully understand?

PRIZE DAY

Can we think of a better way to reward our children
than inviting the six most compliant pupils
to stand on the stage
with a false grin, like they were told,
holding the certificate upright,
facing forwards, until they are dismissed
with a nod of the head – applause
for doing what we asked,
what was required?
Uniform – check,
hair tidy – check,
quiet when I asked once, not twice – check.
Sit up straight,
eyes on me,
do as I say.
Might there be another way?

Could we reward our children
for spirit,
for the sparkle in their eye,
for passion, imagination,
curiosity, great questions asked,
insuppressible energy,
a genuine smile
as they can't resist sharing a joke with the child next to them,
even though the whole school is watching?

TRAFFIC

Gridlock in Lusaka –
a busy crossroads where the traffic lights stopped working long ago;
a Tetris box filled with lorries, minibuses, cars, trucks,
at right angles to each other with no room to move. Stuck.
Drivers turn off their engines.
People emerge gradually, patiently assessing the situation.
One waves his arms, "If you move a little, they go forward,
and you move back.
Yes, like that."
Vehicles obey,
and after not too long
we move.
No horns blaring.
It's not a blame game –
who would we blame anyway?
This is stepping up, taking responsibility.
We are the traffic.
We'll resolve it together.

THE WILD

A long time ago
there was a leopard
in a tree in the hospital courtyard –
a busy mission hospital;
people walk for days to be treated there.
I wonder who looked up and spotted
its beautiful tawny patterned fur, golden-green eyes,
powerful claws; what they thought;
how long until it attacked?
They darted and released the leopard,
but the story stayed with me –
how close the wild is,
no matter how much we try to control,
and how it can get in
and reach us
where we least expect it.

CREATIVITY

Thoughts fly by,
swirl all around us all.
Will we see them?
Catch them as they pass,
squash them like a mosquito –
impotent, powerless
a dark mess.
Or deny their existence?
Push them down
with distractions,
endless distractions,
so that we don't hear the call
of what is truly ours,
don't heed the voice
calling "'Here I am"
but deny the inevitable
until we can no longer say
"I didn't know."
Because the waves crash about our heads,
until we know.

SCHOOL

As you enter the school
and look up,
there's a display of children's paintings,
and it says
in big lettering,
"Don't quack like a duck,
soar like an eagle"'
and I always think
"What if you're a duck?"
Can we celebrate
the quack
from a beautiful duck
who might just be the change
we need
too?

WHITES AT THE ROBOTS*

"One day there might be whites at the robots."
We like to say,
"If you can see it,
you can be it" –
imagine the cracks,
the self-doubt,
to go from Madame, Bwana to that –
begging for food,
if they look
like
you.

* traffic lights

"One day there might be whites at the robots." –
A phrase suggesting that one day the level of poverty
for some white people might mean they need to beg
alongside poor Zambians at the traffic lights in Lusaka.

CRY

Don't cry to the bags of charcoal
that were trees –
they have a new purpose now,
but we still need to breathe,
need the soil to stay,
not be washed far away with the rains
leaving red dust,
and giant baobab trees floating above
their exposed roots of sheer drops
where there used to be land.

Don't cry to the lake
or the dried-up well –
they tried to keep up with all that change
but the groundwater wasn't being replenished,
and could you stay clear and balanced
with the chemicals, sewage, plastic,
left to rot and circulate in every living thing?

No, cry to the smoky sky, to the burning hills,
soar like an eagle over what remains.
Where will our help come from,
when it's almost too late,
but we hope there is
still time?

COMPLICATED

When I first came to Zambia
I wanted to help,
and it took a while to see
that it was complicated.
The NGO were stealing everything,
money diverted to their farms
instead of the villagers living in the most remote areas
up the lake.
So I tried my best where I could,
built relationships;
I look back and they probably
had the biggest impact
over the help.
Sixteen years later, I so want to help,
and I do a little –
a school uniform here,
school books there, a bag of mealie meal,
and then I kick myself
when people stop me in the street.
I have put myself back there.
When will I learn?
But there is also a need –
people are hungry,
there aren't simple answers.
You can do too much and too little
and not enough,
so I wrestle with the same questions, over and over
and decide, however complicated,
I'll try to keep my heart
open.

UNDERSTANDING

What I've learned is that right and wrong,
black and white thinking leads to
'*His* fault...'
'*She* always...'
'*They* caused all this hurt.'

When it feels
juicy,
rewarding,
or fixating,
the best thing to do
is to step your mind away.
It's not true,
never true –
so little is *always* true
about us complicated humans.

The key,
if we can catch it as it flies compellingly through the air
before it lands with a loud clang that vibrates through our souls,
is to feel that juice,
that delicious self-righteousness
and put it back where it came from.

Only then
will there be peace.

DISCOVERIES

I had no idea
that most people see pictures
in their mind
until very recently.
Counting sheep is such an effort,
it seemed counterintuitive
to make your mind say –
there goes a sheep, jumping over the fence. One.
Oh, and there's another. Two.
How could I ever go to sleep
using all that energy?
And I never knew people just
watch those sheep.
Aren't we fascinating?
I've always used words
to fix images, or memories,
because the picture won't stay –
the beauty,
the light,
the joy I feel
seeing the children tumbling like puppies
when all the world feels ok,
as it should be.
Emotions, words, movement, setting, thoughts
make a snapshot to treasure, as rich as possible,
without the image,
always without the image.

HE CAME BACK

He came back
full of cuddles and touch,
clinging a little
to joy and pleasure and appreciation
as if,
having looked at death,
there was more to squeeze
out of life.

ESCARPMENT

The road weaves, sandwiched
by red-tinged golden grasses, still-green trees
and hills in all directions.
Some angular, some softly rounded,
covered in nothing but grass and trees.

Back to the road,
and potholes like small craters.
A tyre lies abandoned.
A Land Cruiser comes into view ahead of us,
slowed to a crawl behind a fuel tanker whose
brakes
might
fail.

We are going down,
ears popping down to the valley,
and off the plateau to the river.
Small huts with thatch appear, cows and goats,
and charcoal for sale on displays of logs.
The river is dry again.

Branches on the road warn of a broken-down truck.
There's the first baobab tree – majestic.

I've heard stories of men with ropes,
who climb onto the back of trucks
as they struggle up the escarpment.
By the time they reach the top,
the trucks are empty.

A family of baboons appear as the shadows lengthen.
As we wind along the road at top speed now,
avoiding obstacles like in a video game –
there are no jack-knifed trucks across the road
today.

SKYDIVING

We jumped out of a plane.
It felt like a dream –
the falling fast, down, down,
then floating above an island
of white sandy beaches and emerald sea,
landing in the soft sand.

I spent much of my time
sky falling, floating,
worrying if my son was alright.
Perhaps he wasn't,
and now, what have I done?

There he was, above me,
floating under a blue parachute.
We landed, laughing, happy,
challenged and triumphant,
but this responsibility of parenting
follows me as I fall-float through life,
never knowing if I pushed too far, too little,
or just enough.

THE RAINS

The rains
thunder steadily,
closer now.
The flash of lightning
over there.
You see the defined edges
of the sheet of rain –
steel grey
and vertical,
a curtain of downpour.

A few fat, heavy drops of rain start,
followed by a deluge.
Rain hammers on the roof,
thunder claps in your ears,
all so loud.

Lightning illuminates it all for a split second
and is gone. Drama.
Potholes and ditches fill in minutes,
turning to waterfalls, streams, gushing rivers,
and you find yourself asking
if the roof will hold.

As quickly as it came, it's quiet,
except for the gushing,
the rushing of the water,
and the birds.

Inswa come with the rains.
They fly blindly,
their long, elegant wings
flittering and fluttering.

If you are hungry at night,
shine a torch towards a bucket filled with water.
The inswa fly in.
Pull off their wings,
and fry them
like popcorn.

CONFIDENCE

Maybe you think the world owes you something.
Maybe you worry you'll achieve nothing.
Maybe you think there are countries, continents waiting for
  your brilliance,
or maybe you're scared that you won't have a place.
Whichever it is, know that confidence isn't gained through
  waiting.
Perhaps no one will invite you to step up.

So listen to your heart,
and take a step that means something to you,
without being invited, without being asked,
without the confidence of knowing
that you're going to do well,
or that anyone cares.
The next right step –
take it.

If that goes well, keep on going.
If it's not quite right, make a change,
and eventually you will grow.
Confidence, elusive confidence is gained
through scary steps, one step at a time,
in tune with your heart.

Don't wait to be invited – try.
Call it play, call it an experiment;
do what's in your heart.
These are the building blocks of a life –
your life.

WAVES

Acceptance like the ocean,
like the waves.
Movement in different directions
becomes a wave,
a half wave,
a wave that didn't become as much as it might have been.
Two waves joined, unexpected,
this moment just right for power, height, momentum, majesty.
Or rocks push sideways, side waves
merge, interact, no blame,
simply waves and movement,
becoming the big wide sea
for another round before the next without end.
A changing myriad of factors –
wind, tide, obstacles
lead to what is,
always what is.

DUSK

Half light,
neither day nor night.
An oversized full moon
like a globe suspended in the sky –
lilac orange yellow
glow.
Red earth,
fires starting to be lit –
the smell mingles with the dust.
Dusk –
the time in between
smells like a blanket, comforting,
like something lost
and found again.

SAVANNAH

My daughter was named for our connection to this place.
We didn't know if we'd be back
but we knew it had meant something.
Her accent oscillates, fluctuates
without noticing, effortlessly shifting
between cultures, continents.
How do we show the layers on our hearts?
Is it names, pronunciation, clothing, tattoos, scars,
photos in a frame?
What calls us to publicly declare –
I was here
and it changed me?

CHOICES

The richness of life
is never one thing –
responsibility and limitations,
grief alongside relief,
freedom.
To experience connection
we must clip our wings a little.
Love is considering someone else,
their needs, and feelings.
We can choose,
and if we're lucky
we get to fly a little together
and experience the magic of adventure,
before we find ourselves
a little later down the road of life,
a clump of red earth in one hand,
and a piece of brilliant blue sky
in the other. A choice.

ENDINGS

Will this all feel like a dream?
London is not Lusaka. There will be no monkeys
jumping from branch to branch
at the end of our road, nor this pink light
either side of a hot, harsh sun.
We'll fit back in.
Which parts of us will remember the place
where we didn't quite fit?

GLOSSARY

The bush – a large, undeveloped area of land

Bwana – boss, from Swahili

Chitenge – colourful African fabric often worn by women, wrapped around the chest or waist, over the head as a headscarf, or as a baby sling. Both men and women wear chitenge outfits for formal occasions or traditional celebrations

Inswa – flying termites that come out during the rainy season

Kapenta – small fish, also called Tanganyika sardines, found in Lake Kariba

Kwacha – Zambian currency

Masau – a fruit grown on trees (Ziziphus Mauritania) also known as 'Indian Jujube', 'Chinese Apple', or 'Indian Plum'

Mealie meal – dried ground maize used to make nshima

NGO – Non-governmental organisation - a non-profit organisation, typically addressing social or political issues

Nshima – Zambian staple food, thick porridge made from ground maize

Relish – meat, fish, beans or vegetables served alongside nshima

Robots – traffic lights

Tonga – one of Zambia's 72 languages, a Bantu language mainly spoken by the Tonga people

ZESCO – Zambian state-owned national power company

BIOS

Rachel Davies is from London, UK, and discovered her love of writing poetry while spending time in Lusaka, Zambia. She has a degree in theology and religious studies from Cambridge University, and originally travelled to Zambia for a year with Voluntary Services Overseas (VSO) when she was 24. She went on to train at Le Cordon Bleu before running Rachel's Kitchen Cookery School for over a decade. Most recently, she trained as a coach, and works in leadership development and coaching, alongside other creative projects.

Rachel is currently back in London with her husband and their two children, plotting their next adventure. *Life, In Shorts* is her first published book of poetry.

Cover image by Natasha Evans

Born in Zimbabwe and raised from a young age in Zambia, Natasha Evans moved to England in her early twenties to study art. After completing her BA Hons Degree in illustration she returned to Zambia, where she lives with her husband and four children in Lusaka. Natasha creates contemporary mixed media works as well as limited edition prints and functional art pieces in her purpose-built studio. She has a particular interest in the city of Lusaka and is intrigued by the buildings and their relationship to the people who live in the urban landscape. Natasha's work more broadly focuses on ideas relating to concepts of home, belonging, and travel.

AFTERWORD + ACKNOWLEDGEMENTS

I wanted to share my experiences as honestly as I could, and that includes some of the messy parts of life, including inequality and corruption. I appreciate that writing about these topics might not sit well with many people - myself included - but it is also part of life in Zambia. Perhaps things will change, but for now, they are part of today's reality.

I am also conscious of looking in from the outside, which is in part what made our time in Zambia so energising. Seeing places and cultures with fresh eyes, for me, makes everything fascinating.

I am aware that I was an outsider in a place that historically has been used by colonial powers, people with power and money, and I hope that I am honouring the place, culture and people, and sharing my experiences without taking more than I gave.

I'm very grateful to everyone who welcomed us and helped us settle into our new lives - Emily, Ash, Valentina, Tabea, Francis, Demi, Gareth, Charles, Miriam, Amanda, Elly, Rivky, Mendy, the Evans family and so many others.

To Tash, Piers, Indie, Jess, Zac and Rafe for welcoming us into your lives and beautiful home, for your friendship, and to Tash for sharing your incredible art on the cover. To Rhoda and Wizas for making us feel at home.

Crystal, Jason, Carla, Rainer, Mouse, Cilla, Annari, Gert, Steph, Alex, Melissa, Hein and kiddies for your friendship and warm welcomes every time we come back to the most beautiful place in the world.

Katie, Sister Purity and Naomi at Brighter Futures Zambia for our trip to the villages around Monze. The work you do is incredible.

Thank you also to everyone who helped during the process of writing and collating this collection - Jacqueline, Fern, Carol-Anne, Mo, Julia, David, Nao, Maggie, Poppy, Ali, Mitch, Annette, Sarah, James, Linda, and in loving memory of Anthea - thank you for helping me to share this, and for your friendship. I needed your gentle encouragement to move past the fear.

To VSO for sending me to Zambia all those years ago, and to friends and family who make life full.

Jo and Simon, Dee and Greg, Noam, Lia, Yoav - you're the best. And to my parents for your gentle encouragement and patience every time I leave. Goethe said parents should give their children roots and wings, and I'm grateful for both.

To Savannah and Teddy for coming along for the ride - experiencing it all through your eyes and seeing the joy you get is pure happiness for me. And to Simon, for fully embracing my ideas, sharing yours, and helping turn it all into our adventures, I love you.